A gift For:

_____

From:

_____

✝THE
PROMISE

A Christmas Tale by
TED DEKKER

COUNTRYMAN

NASHVILLE, TENNESSEE

Copyright © 2005 by Ted Dekker

Published by J. Countryman®, a division of the Thomas Nelson, Inc.,
Nashville, Tennessee 37214

All rights reserved. No portion of this publication may be reproduced,
stored in a retrieval system, or transmitted by any means—electronic,
mechanical, photocopying, recording, or any other—except for brief
quotations in printed reviews, without the prior written permission of
the publisher.

J. Countryman® is a trademark of Thomas Nelson, Inc.

Project Editor: Kathy Baker

Designed by Koechel Peterson & Associates, Minneapolis, Minnesota

ISBN 1-4041-0233-7

Printed and bound in the United States of America

www.jcountryman.com | www.thomasnelson.com

www.teddekker.com

LIKE THIS BOY,
MAY YOU SING OF LIGHT,
EVEN WHEN NO ONE ELSE
CAN HEAR.

ONCE UPON A TIME in a land called
Palestine there lived a boy named Reuben. But
Reuben wasn't an ordinary boy. Not ordinary at
all, unless being special, as most children are, is
ordinary. Then you might say Reuben was quite
ordinary, because he was very special.

He looked like a normal boy with his round
face and dimpled cheeks and ruffled brown hair.
He walked like a normal boy and could even run
faster than most of the older children, although he
was only ten.

Reuben was smart and he was very kind and he should have been loved by everyone who ever met him.

Instead, he was hated.

The others in the tribe didn't use the word "hate," of course, not with his mother nearby to scold them. But Reuben knew he was hated by the way they looked at him with glaring eyes and by the way they spit on the ground when he passed by.

He was hated because he was an orphan. And he was hated because he couldn't speak.

If it wasn't for Naomi, who'd found him abandoned near a village and raised him as her only son, Reuben was sure the tribe would have left him to die in the desert a long time ago.

Even Naomi's husband, Jude, who was also the leader of the traveling tribe, disliked him.

He'd beaten Reuben with a stick once, groaning through terrible tears that Naomi was mocking him by allowing an orphan mute to squat in their tent when they didn't have their own son.

"But God has given us a son!" Naomi cried, throwing herself at Jude to save her son.

"There is no God who would curse us with a mute!" Jude said.

If not for his mother's love, Reuben would have died a dozen deaths in his ten short years. She was his savior.

And now she was being taken from him.

Reuben stood trembling in the tent, staring at his mother's form on the bed. Listening to her ragged breaths, he was sure that she couldn't last through the night.

His mother was dying.

I beg you, God in heaven, to heal my mother, he cried in his mind. *Please, I beg you. Take my eyes, or my legs, or whatever you want, but please don't take my mother.*

Naomi suddenly gasped. Her eyes glistened in the lamplight, wide in surprise or pain, he couldn't tell which.

Mama?

"Reuben?" She spoke his name at the ceiling. Did she know he was here?

He took a tentative step forward. *Mama, I'm here!* He was screaming the words, but she couldn't hear. He was mute.

Naomi suddenly turned her head toward him, and although she was weak, her face shone with an energy that seemed miraculous.

"Reuben! Reuben, come!" She grasped his arm with a trembling hand. Her face wrinkled and tears leaked from her eyes.

"My sweet boy, I have heard from God!"

God?

Naomi took a deep breath because now even

breathing took great effort.

"There is a king coming . . ." Another breath. "He will take you in. You must find him. They won't know that he's a king. But you must find him. You must . . ."

She was talking fast now. Frantic. And her strength was quickly fading.

"Find him, Reuben. Find him and lead the others to him. Then he will give you a voice to praise him."

Give me my voice? How can that be? How will I know him?

Reuben was asking the questions in his mind as he always did, but he'd forgotten that she couldn't hear him. He picked up the tablet from the bed-side table, wrote out the question, and showed it to her.

He could see the light dim in her eyes. She was dying!

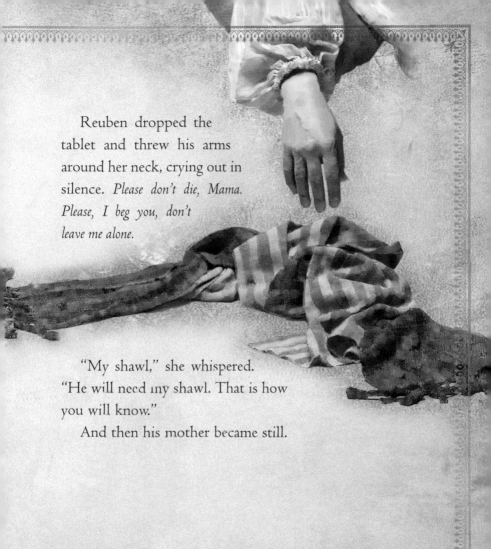

Reuben dropped the tablet and threw his arms around her neck, crying out in silence. *Please don't die, Mama. Please, I beg you, don't leave me alone.*

"My shawl," she whispered. "He will need my shawl. That is how you will know."

And then his mother became still.

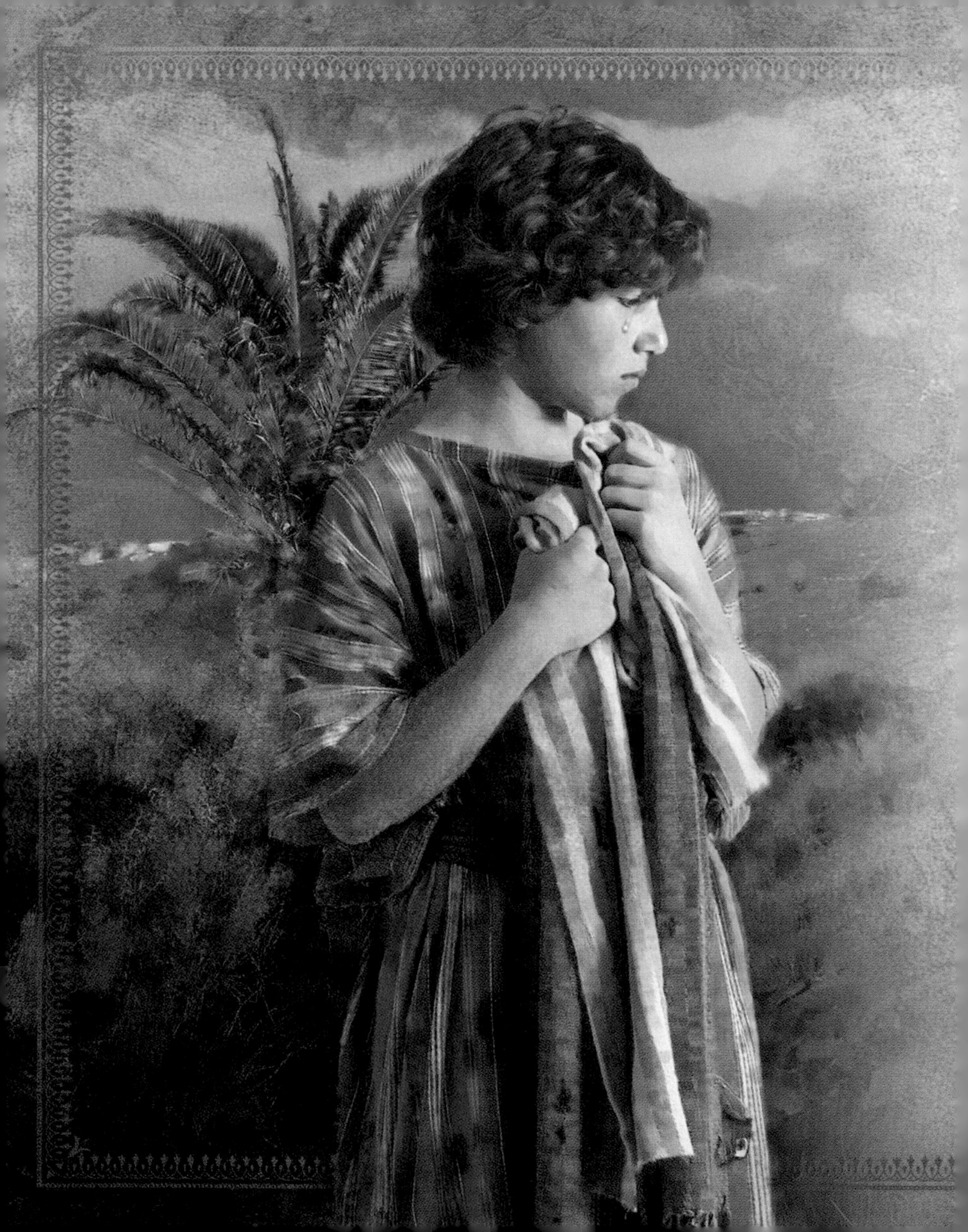

THE TRIBE buried Naomi the next day, and no one wept as long or as bitterly as Reuben did. The others looked at him disapprovingly, as if they wished it was he rather than Naomi being buried. Jude, now his guardian by tribal law, ignored him altogether.

The only thing Reuben now had was Naomi's promise and the shawl, which he soaked with his tears and clutched tightly wherever he went. As his heart quieted, Reuben began to put his hope in his mother's dying words. He had to find this king.

He hadn't heard the voice of God himself. In fact he wasn't even so sure that there was a God. But his mother said that she'd heard God's voice, and so Reuben would believe her—he had no one else to believe now.

He would offer the shawl to every stranger who came to the camp, even if they didn't look like a king, because his mother had said the rest wouldn't know he was a king. One of them would be a king who would take the shawl. The king would sweep Reuben into his arms and heal his voice, and the whole camp would be amazed that anyone should love the orphan boy as much as the king did.

Reuben returned to tending the horses as he always did. He avoided the shepherds as much as possible and kept to himself in the tent, eating what Jude left for him to eat and sleeping in the corner behind a slip of canvas as he always had.

At any sign that a visitor might be approaching, Reuben ran outside and peered longingly at the horizon. But none came.

One day an older girl who had always mocked him walked over to where he was brushing a horse.

"Why do you carry your mama's shawl around with you?" Esther demanded. "Don't you know it makes you look pathetic? You should run away now."

Reuben decided then to keep the shawl hidden in the ground under his mat.

A week later, travelers rode into camp. Three men on horses looking very stately indeed. Could one of them be a king?

Reuben ran to his mat, threw back the corner, and yanked out the shawl. Heart beating like hoofs, he tore outside, across the camp, right up to the first traveler who was still seated on a large black horse.

Reuben thrust the shawl up toward the man.

Please, my king, accept my gift to you, he cried in his mind. *Accept it and I will worship you with a voice that will echo across the whole earth.*

But the stranger didn't move to accept the shawl.

Only then did Reuben realize he was standing at the center of a large circle that had gathered to welcome the travelers.

Laughter filled his ears.

"Do I look like I need your rag?" the man on the horse asked, and he too began to laugh. The other two travelers joined him.

Reuben's heart sank into his stomach. His face flushed with embarrassment and he backed away, filled with shame. The moment he cleared the ring of shepherds he ran for home, burst through the flap, and flung the shawl on the floor.

I've been a fool! What kind of king would need a dirty shawl? My mother was hearing voices as she died. I am lost!

He threw himself on his mat and cried.

But by the end of the day he'd strengthened his courage and decided that his mother had heard from God after all. This was his only hope.

He wouldn't be discouraged by a few laughs. He would offer the shawl to the next visitor no matter what the others said.

This time his wait lasted only three days. A band of travelers, eight in all, walked into camp from the south, herding a small flock of sheep.

His previous failure nearly forgotten, Reuben retrieved the shawl and once again ran to meet the guests. He thrust the strip of cloth out and bowed his head.

Please accept my gift, oh king. Please, I beg you. Be the king sent by God to . . .

"Away, boy!" The lead man slapped his hands and the shawl fell to the ground.

Before Reuben knew what was happening, Esther had scooped up the shawl. She tossed it to one of the boys, who ran off with it.

Reuben had taken three steps after the older boy,

terrified that he might lose his mother's shawl, when Jude grabbed him by the tunic and flung him down.

"What foolishness is this, boy?"

Still afraid that he might lose the shawl, Reuben scrambled to his knees and scrawled in the dust

A KING. THE SHAWL IS FOR A KING.

"He thinks a king will save him!" someone cried. Laughter broke out.

"Who told you this nonsense?" Jude demanded.

Again he scrawled.

GOD.

"God? There is no God, you little . . ."

Reuben bolted before Jude could grab him again. He found the children at the animal pens where they'd hidden the shawl.

Closing his ears to the children's teasing, Reuben retrieved the dirty shawl and ran home. He washed it carefully and set it out to dry beside his bed.

That night he slept with it against his chest, and he sang himself silently to sleep.

My king, my king, please find me and save me.
Save me and I will forever sing your praise.

I am lost without you, my king, my king.
Put me on your horse and take me to your kingdom
where I will sing to you in your palace while all the
people watch.

Two weeks passed before the next visitors rode into their camp. This time Reuben stood behind the crowd with the shawl hidden under his tunic, then slowly pulled it out and lifted the shawl over his head until he was sure that the riders had seen it. They looked at him without any reaction, then moved on.

Reuben slipped the shawl back under his tunic and retreated to his tent with a heavy heart.

He had just lifted his bedroll to hide the shawl when the tent flap flew open.

"Give it to me!" Jude snapped, stomping across the room.

He shoved Reuben aside and snatched up the

shawl. "Our code may require that I provide for you because my late wife demanded it when she died, but it makes no mention of my putting up with an imbecile. You won't embarrass me again. This rag will be burnt!"

Terrified by the prospect, Reuben leapt for the shawl, got one hand on it, and came away with a small fistful of torn cloth.

Jude's hand struck Reuben's face broadside, sending him flying back to the ground. "Try that again and I will be in my rights to leave you in a deep hole when we break camp tomorrow."

Reuben scrambled for his tablet. He couldn't lose the shawl. And he couldn't leave the camp. A king was coming.

He was screaming in protest, but only a soft moan came from his throat. Still, it was enough to make Jude pause.

Reuben wrote as quickly as he could in his panic.

GIVE ME THE CLOTH AND I WILL NEVER
LEAVE THE TENT DURING THE DAY.

He flipped the tablet around to face Jude. For a long time the tribe's elder studied him. He finally tossed the shawl at Reuben's feet.

"Then consider this pathetic little tent your prison. You'll care for the horses at night and stay here by day. Cross the threshold and I will burn the rag."

Jude marched from the tent.

Reuben dropped on the small torn shawl, pulled it into his belly, and curled up in a ball.

He would never part with the shawl. Not as long as he lived. Not until it was taken by a king who would give him a new life.

LITTLE REUBEN kept his promise to the leader by staying in the tent during the day and caring for the horses by night.

He often peered from the doorway, looking for travelers as they came and went. When he saw one, he would pull back the flap and hold up the shawl for them to see, but none of them paid attention to the boy holding a rag. Still, Reuben kept his hope alive by singing silent songs of love to the king who would one day rescue him.

A year passed. Then two. Many visitors came and went. The band of shepherds traveled farther south and met many travelers along the way. Whenever visitors came, Reuben hurried to the edge of the tent and held up his shawl, hoping they would glance his way and see it. The camp soon spoke of him as the boy who had lost his mother and with her, his mind.

One evening, as Reuben was preparing to tend to the horses, Jude came into the tent. The man rarely spoke to Reuben, but something clearly was on his mind.

"I've decided that you may be of some good to us, after all," he said. "I've just come from the town over the hill, and it's crowded with travelers. You will go tonight and earn your keep. Beg, steal, find some desperate fool who will pay you for work—I don't care. But don't come back without a fistful of coins. Do you understand?"

And so it was that Reuben left the band of shepherds for the first time in his memory and headed over the hill toward the flickering lights of the nearby town.

He'd cleaned his shoes and put on a clean tunic and folded the shawl into his belt for safe keeping.

The sounds of voices carried to him while he was still a good way off, and he considered running back to the camp. But he couldn't find the stomach to face Jude empty-handed.

He wouldn't steal, although thieving was a respectable enough livelihood among the tribes. He didn't know how to beg and even if he did, he didn't think he could subject himself to the humiliation it would bring.

But he could mind a stable.

Reuben stopped at the town's edge and stared at the streets. So many people, even now after dark. Did they all live in this town? Surely not.

Everywhere he looked he saw travelers leading donkeys piled high with boxes and bags. How could he find work without asking for it? And how could he ask if he was a mute?

   He finally worked up the courage to enter the
town. With so many travelers no one would pay

him any mind. At first he walked with his head down, so that he wouldn't have to look anyone in the eye. But when no one stopped him he became more confident and studied the town in awe as he walked.

People everywhere, talking excitedly, arguing endlessly, going somewhere. Houses and inns of all kinds. Each of the inns had a stable where travelers could leave their horses for the night as they slept.

Reuben approached the nearest stable and poked his head into the stalls.

"Stay away from the animals!" a voice snapped from behind.

Reuben spun around and faced a man carrying a bale of hay.

"Are you deaf? Get away!"

He hurried to the street and walked a long way before gathering the courage to try another stable.

Three men were drinking and laughing in this one. Maybe boys didn't tend stables in the towns. Why would they hire a boy when plenty of men needed the work?

But Reuben had no choice. He had to earn a fistful of coins.

The next four stables were cleaned, stocked, and the animals already bedded down. No need for help.

Reuben walked the streets for over an hour before he came to an inn on the farthest side of town. Like all of the inns, its stable was behind the main building. But he knew as soon as he neared that someone was already working in this stable.

He could hear the voices. A man talking quickly in hushed tones. A woman crying softly.

He was already turning around when the woman suddenly cried out. She was in pain?

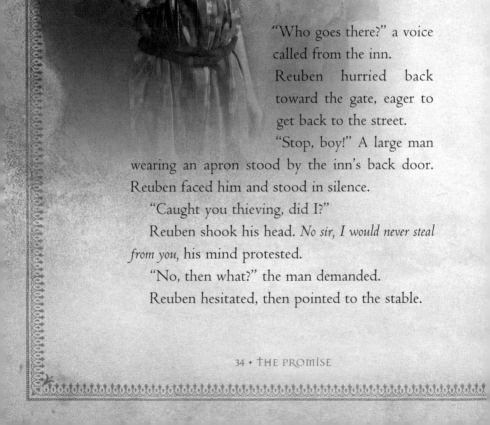

"Who goes there?" a voice called from the inn.

Reuben hurried back toward the gate, eager to get back to the street.

"Stop, boy!" A large man wearing an apron stood by the inn's back door. Reuben faced him and stood in silence.

"Caught you thieving, did I?"

Reuben shook his head. *No sir, I would never steal from you,* his mind protested.

"No, then what?" the man demanded.

Reuben hesitated, then pointed to the stable.

"Speak up. Have you lost your tongue?"

Reuben knew the man didn't mean the question in earnest, but he nodded anyway.

"You're a mute?"

Again, he nodded.

The man's face settled in kindness. He glanced at the stables. "God knows I could use some help. Can you tend to animals?"

Reuben nodded, eagerly this time.

"Tend to the animals and I'll give you something in the morning. Do you have a place to sleep?"

Reuben shook his head. *No.*

"Then I suppose you can sleep in the stables. There's already a man and his wife out there; try to stay out of their way."

Reuben stared at the man, unsure of what to do next.

"Well, go on then. Get to work."

Reuben ran to the stables, thrilled by the sudden turn of good fortune. But as soon as he entered the first stall, the sound of the woman's crying stopped him short. There were a dozen stalls in the stables, then a door at the end. A granary or a special stall maybe. The cries of pain were coming from the far room.

A horse snorted softly. These were Reuben's stables to care for tonight. Mama would be proud.

The woman cried softly again. Perhaps he should make sure she was all right. Just a peek.

Reuben was halfway to the door when a man in a long dirtied tunic rushed out. He stopped when he saw Reuben.

"Water, boy. Do you know where I can find more water?"

Reuben pointed to a trough.

"That'll never do. I need clean water. She's having the baby!"

The man rushed by, headed for the inn.

Growing up in a camp, Reuben had heard the sounds of childbirth before, but he'd never been this close. He eased up to the stall and peered through the doorway. A single lamp lit the tiny room. They'd made a bed from straw on one side. There lay a young woman, holding her stomach, face glistening with sweat.

It was frightening to see a woman in so much pain. And so alone. Normally nursemaids or sisters huddled around a tent when a woman was going to give birth. But this was just one woman on a straw bed.

He glanced around. A single donkey stood in the nearest stall, looking at him dumbly. Silent. Two sheep were tethered to a post. A goat was chewing the bark on one of the posts, ignoring them all. One of the sheep suddenly bleated, and Reuben jumped.

The woman glanced at the door, saw him, then rolled slightly, groaning in pain.

"Get back, boy."

The man had returned with a basin of sloshing water. Reuben stepped to one side, afraid he might be struck for his indiscretion, but the man walked past without another word. Then he was speaking in soft comforting words to his wife.

Reuben quickly retreated to the other end of the stables, set the shawl on a post where it would be safe, and began caring for a horse that stamped nervously. He rubbed the animal's neck and pushed a palmful of oats to its muzzle.

The woman's cries came and went over the next hour as Reuben tended to the guests' animals, one by one. Just about the time he managed to return his mind to his work, the woman would cry out and send a shiver down his back. Had his birth mother suffered this much to bring him into the world? Surely she had. If he was ever fortunate enough to meet her, Reuben would kiss her feet for enduring such an awful ordeal.

The cries suddenly grew more terrible, accompanied by groans and the steady encouragement from the husband.

"Almost, Mary. Just once more. Don't give up!"

There was one loud, long cry that Reuben was sure would bring the neighbors running, then a loud, "It's done!" from the man.

The mother began to sob softly.

"It's a boy!" the man said. "A boy, I tell you, just as he said."

Reuben grabbed his shawl, clutched it as if it might offer him security, then edged toward the stable door.

A baby's cry cut through the night.

"A boy!" the man cried again, as only a proud father could.

"He needs to be kept warm." The mother. "Give him to me, Joseph. Give me my baby and get something soft to warm him."

"I've used the clothing . . . I'll find something."

Joseph barged from the stall. Reuben now stood just ten paces from the door. The man's eyes glanced over him and stopped on the shawl.

"The shawl is yours?"

The shawl? Reuben didn't think to respond.

"It looks clean enough. We've been on a very long journey and haven't had time to wash our clothing. I had to use what we had for the birth. Could I use your shawl?"

Reuben was too stunned to respond. This man had just asked for his shawl! What did that mean? Was this man the king?

"Please, I will return it in the morning, but we need it now. My wife has just given birth to a baby. A boy!"

Reuben held the shawl out.

The moment Joseph clasped his hand around the cloth, the weight of the moment descended on Reuben as if the sky itself had fallen.

He had found his king! This man was the king.

Reuben collapsed on the ground and lay face down with his arms stretched forward as far as he could reach them in worship. A sob wracked his body.

Silence filled the stables. Joseph stood still, then stepped back.

"The shawl is for the boy," he said. Then he turned and hurried into the stall.

Reuben scrambled to his knees. The boy? The shawl was needed by the boy, not Joseph! His mother had said that the king would need the shawl.

The baby was the king!

He pushed himself to his feet and stumbled

into the stall. They were wrapping the baby in the shawl. Mary pulled the baby close, kissed his head, and rocked him gently.

Reuben sank to his knees, clenched his eyes, clasped his hands together.

You are my king to whom I will sing. Forever I will serve you, for you have come to save me.

He sang it loudly, but not a sound came from his mouth. His mother's promise strung through his mind. *Find him and lead the others to him. Then he will give you a voice to praise him.*

Reuben's eyes snapped open. He knew what he must do. The mother and father looked at him with blank stares. They neither scolded him, nor encouraged him. Did they know their son was a king?

Reuben would have said something if he'd had a voice, but anything he might try to explain

by tablet now would take far too long. He had
to return to the camp tonight. He had to make
Jude understand.

Reuben left Mary and
Joseph staring and ran
for the hills.

IT TOOK Reuben half an hour to reach the fields where the camp lay. He was running fast, but in his mind he felt like he was flying.

He'd found the king! And he could prove it. The child needed his shawl.

Never mind that it could just be a coincidence. Sure, all babies needed swaddling clothes, but which baby would need a shawl that Naomi had said he would need more than two years ago?

A king, that's who.

The fires were out and the camp was asleep

when Reuben reached his tent. He threw the flap
wide and ran for his tablet.

> THE KING IS HERE! YOU MUST FOLLOW
> ME TO SEE THE KING.

Even as he wrote it his heart began to fall. Who
would take him seriously in the camp? No one!
Still, he had to try.
He hurried to Jude's sleeping form, nudged the
man, and held up the tablet.

Jude groaned and turned over.

Reuben tried again, pushing the leader harder this time. *Wake up, wake up, Jude! You have to wake up!*

Jude sat up and stared at the tablet. Then at Reuben.

"You have coins?"

Coins?

Jude struck the tablet from his hand. "Get out! Don't come back without coins or you'll feel the whip. Now go!"

Reuben scooped up the tablet and ran outside. He was beyond himself with panic now. The camp lay in total silence. If he didn't lead them to the stable tonight, he might never find the baby again. Surely the mother and father wouldn't stay in the stable more than one night!

God in heaven who spoke to my mother, Naomi, be my voice now, he cried. *Wake the dead. Make the blind see and the deaf hear and give me a voice. If you don't I will die. I will surely die.*

There would be shepherds watching over the sheep for the night on the far side of the camp, but they were the hardest of all men. He had to wake the women. Better the whole camp.

Horses, he thought. *I'll use the horses!*

Reuben tucked the tablet into his belt and ran for the corral. He pulled the gate open, snatched up a stick, and gathered the horses into one group.

He led one of the stallions to the camp's edge with the others close behind, fifteen in all. Then he struck the horse on the rump with the stick.

It bolted forward.

Reuben ran behind the others, striking each as he passed. The horses snorted and galloped through the camp, raising a ruckus that was sure to wake everyone.

Reuben ran after them, gripping his tablet.

Tent flaps began to open as horses pounded past. "The horses are loose!" someone yelled.

"Horse thieves!" another voice cried.

Reuben ran to the center before the confusion sent the shepherd camp running in all directions. He shoved his tablet into the air and walked in a circle, showing them all what he'd written.

> THE KING IS HERE! YOU MUST FOLLOW
> ME TO SEE THE KING.

"The boy did it! The fool has set the horses free!"

Reuben spun to the woman who'd raised the warning and jabbed at his tablet. *Please, you must believe me!*

He shoved his arm in the direction of the town, Bethlehem.

"He's gone mad!" the woman cried.

Jude stormed among those who had gathered around Reuben, robe snapping about his ankles with each stride. In his hand he carried a whip that trailed in the dust behind him.

"What have you done? Have you gone completely mad?" He motioned to several of the men. "Get the horses."

Then he bore down on Reuben. "This is it. Tonight you will learn what you should have learned the last time I beat you. Never again, do you hear me? You'll never cause trouble again."

"If you don't I will, Jude," one of the shepherds said. "I swear it on my grave."

Jude held out his whip. "Get down."

Reuben's legs felt so weak from fear that he crumpled to his knees.

"Where is your mother's God now?" Jude drew back the whip. Reuben clenched his eyes.

A flash of light ignited the sky, and Reuben was sure he'd been struck in the head by the whip.

But there was no pain.

He opened his eyes. What he saw made him gasp.

To their right, above the tents, shone a brilliant light that lit the night. And at the center of that light stood a man.

To a man, woman, and child, the shepherds
stood gaping in terror at the sight before them.
But not Reuben. Reuben stared in awe that God

had answered his prayer and come to save him.

"Why are you afraid?" the angel asked. His voice sounded natural enough.

The angel seemed to be looking right at him, as if to say, *You see, there was never any reason to doubt.*

"I bring you good tidings for all people," the angel said. "There is born to you this day in the city of David a Savior who is Christ the Lord."

The angel pointed to Reuben. "And this will be the sign to you." He lowered his arm. "You will find a Babe wrapped in swaddling clothes, lying in a manger."

For a long moment, no one moved. Then Jude dropped to his knees. The whip fell from his hand. His jaw hung open and his eyes were round and Reuben felt a sudden impulse to throw his arms around the man.

But he couldn't move. The angel's light seemed

to hold them all in its grip.

The angel spread his arms, and with that motion the entire night exploded with light. It was as if darkness had been completely destroyed with one silent gesture.

And then it wasn't a silent gesture at all, because suddenly the sky began to sing.

Angels! Thousands of angels, singing from the light, as if they themselves were the light. A powerful, intoxicating refrain that swept over Reuben like a thundering herd of horses.

"Glory to God in the highest;"

Reuben began to shake. He felt a maddening desire to sing with them. To lift his chin and sing this refrain with the angels.

To tell the whole world that his king had been born.

"And on earth peace, goodwill toward men."

Reuben closed his eyes and sang the words at the top of lungs with the angels. He had no voice, of course, but he didn't care anymore.

He was singing to his king! The angels were his voice, and the whole sky was hearing his cry.

"Glory to God in the highest;
And on earth peace, goodwill toward men!"

Time seemed to hold its place as he sang, bathed in the raw power of a hundred thousand angels. He felt as if he himself were floating with them, singing about the Child, the King.

It suddenly occurred to Reuben that only one of the angels now sang. A pure, crystalline voice. Stunningly beautiful. A voice that no one could possibly hear and resist.

He sang on with this one angel. But a change

had come over the night. The light had gone.

Reuben snapped his eyes open.

Stars. A black sky. The angels were gone.

Yet the lone voice still spun its song of praise. Who? Where?

> *"Glory to God in the highest;*
> *And on earth . . ."*

It was the sight of the others on their knees, staring at him, that made Reuben stop singing. The entire tribe was on its knees in the wake of the angel's visit. But now they were looking directly at him.

The song had stopped. A thought occurred to him. Had it been . . . surely it hadn't been he who had sung aloud.

Reuben sang again. Beautiful notes spilled from his mouth.

> *"Glory to God in the highest . . ."*

He could sing?

Something like warm water boiled up through his body to the top of his head. Around him the shepherds were weeping.

He tested his voice. "Hello?" A pure, wonderful sound.

Reuben began to tremble. He pushed himself to his feet. The king had given him a voice!

He threw his arms high, tilted his head back, and began to scream at the sky. "My King, my King, you have made me whole! I will praise you. I will praise you!"

Then he began to sing. He sang the songs that he'd sung so many times in restrained silence. Songs of praise and worship and adoration to the King who had been born this day to save him and the world from the darkest night.

Reuben didn't know how long he sang there on his knees while the shepherds wept uncontrollably around him. But when he finally quieted and rose to his feet, he knew with absolute certainty that the world had just changed.

The tribe looked at him in silence now. Waiting.

He saw that he still held his tablet. He dropped it into the dirt.

"Follow me," he said. "Follow me and we will worship this Child who is wrapped in the shawl given to me by Mother."

He took a deep breath and looked at Jude.

"Follow me and I will show you this King."

Then young Reuben walked into the night, toward Bethlehem, leading the band of shepherds.

When they found Mary and Joseph and the Child lying in the manger, they worshiped him and made widely known the angel's song which was given them concerning this child.

And for as long as he lived, Reuben followed the Christ and sang his praise.

THE END

More from the Mind of Ted Dekker...

With more than a million novels sold and several #1 bestsellers, Ted Dekker is known for mind-bending, adrenaline-laced thrillers, including:

The Martyr's Song

What happens when we begin to hear the song of heaven over the noise of earth…when we long for eternity more than the world we can see? This simple story will forever change how you live out your faith. Includes a CD single by Todd Agnew.

Obsessed

How far would you go to satisfy your deepest obsession? This #1 best-selling novel is the ultimate story of passion, revenge, and an all-consuming obsession for the ultimate treasure.

The Slumber of Christianity: Awakening a Passion for Heaven on Earth

Challenge your mind and deepen your faith with Ted Dekker's first nonfiction book.

Visit TedDekker.com to discover more.